SNAP SHOT™

Senior Editor
Mary Ling

Editor
Caroline Bingham

Art Editor
Joanna Pocock

Designer
Claire Penny

Production
Catherine Semark

Consultant
Phil Wilkinson

A Dorling Kindersley Book

First published in Canada
in 1994 by élan press, an imprint of
General Publishing Co. Limited
30 Lesmill Road, Toronto,
Canada, M3B 2T6

Photography by Geoff Dann, Mike Dunning, John Freeman,
Dave King, Martin Plomer, Jerry Young

Every effort has been made to trace the
copyright holders and we apologise in advance for
any unintentional omissions. We would be pleased to
insert the appropriate acknowledgement in any
subsequent edition of this publication.

CIP data available from the
National Library of Canada
ISBN 1 55144 039 3

Color reproduction by Colourscan
Printed in Belgium by Proost

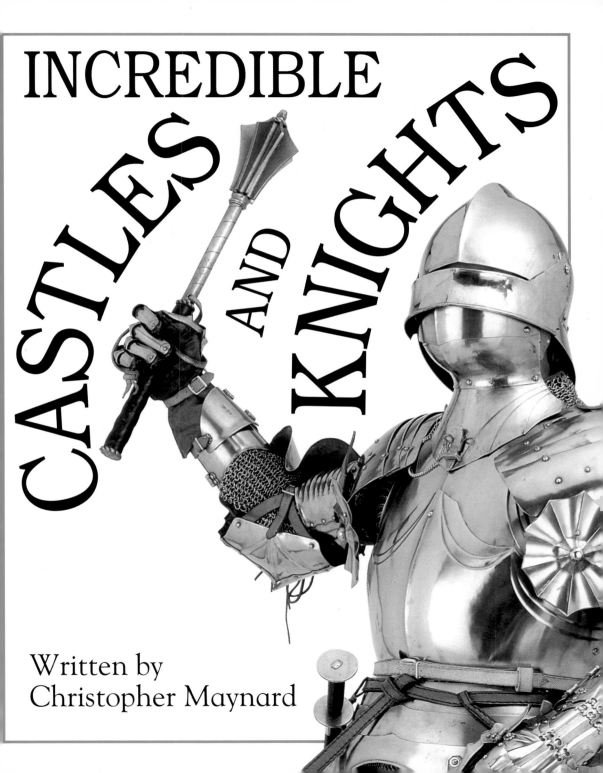

INCREDIBLE
CASTLES
AND
KNIGHTS

Written by
Christopher Maynard

Lord of the manor

Contents

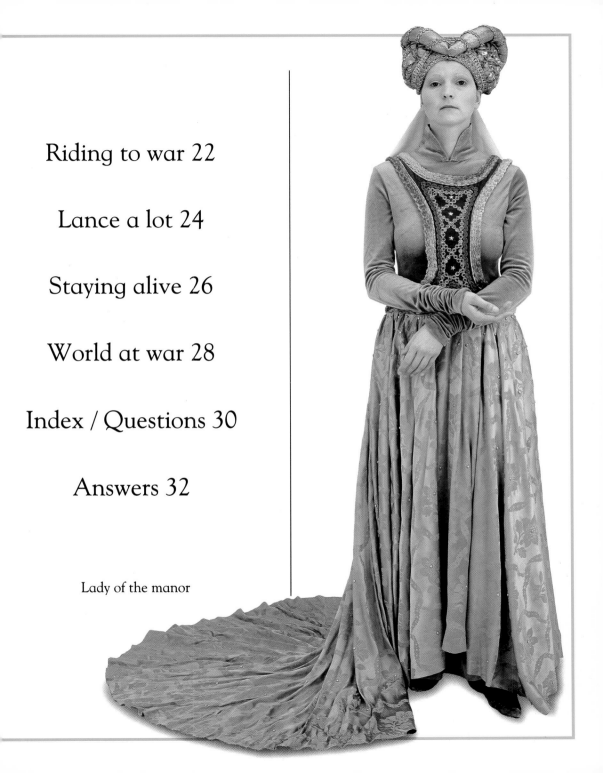

Lady of the manor

Castles and keeps

During the Middle Ages, many rich and powerful lords lived in mighty castles. A castle protected its owner from bands of thieves, rival lords, and invaders from other lands.

An iron-clad wooden portcullis was lowered over the door for extra security.

The slowest way to capture a castle

High towers, called turrets, gave a good view of the enemy's forces.

Soldiers could shoot out from slits in the walls.

In safekeeping
Early stone castles often consisted of just one tower, called a keep. They had incredibly thick walls, and might be 96 ft (35 m) high. Prisoners kept in the keep very rarely escaped!

Fighting to the top
If the main door was built on the second floor, attackers had to force their way up a flight of steps before they could try to break in.

was to starve out the people inside.

The castle gate was guarded by strong towers, a wooden drawbridge, and a portcullis.

The moat kept attackers from digging under the main walls.

Knight time

A knight rode into battle dressed in a suit of armor that would protect him from arrows and sword blows. Armor was not as heavy as it looks – a knight could even run!

Trendy dress
This richly decorated suit of armor was worn for foot combat at tournaments.

The plate armor was made with joints so the knight could move his limbs.

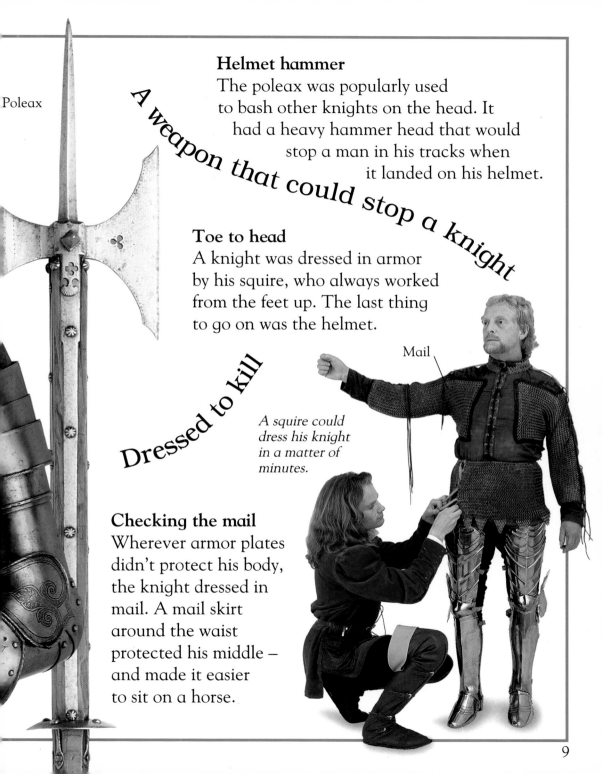

Poleax

Helmet hammer
The poleax was popularly used to bash other knights on the head. It had a heavy hammer head that would stop a man in his tracks when it landed on his helmet.

A weapon that could stop a knight

Toe to head
A knight was dressed in armor by his squire, who always worked from the feet up. The last thing to go on was the helmet.

Mail

Dressed to kill

A squire could dress his knight in a matter of minutes.

Checking the mail
Wherever armor plates didn't protect his body, the knight dressed in mail. A mail skirt around the waist protected his middle – and made it easier to sit on a horse.

9

Castle comforts

Castles were like villages, housing the lord's family, servants, soldiers, and priests. People gathered in the Great Hall for meals and to watch the day's business.

A servant draws yarn from a spinning wheel.

Evenings were spent without television –

Board games

Board games such as checkers and backgammon were popular. Chess was a favorite because it had a mock battlefield where pieces could attack and capture each other.

Children play an old board game called "Foxes and Geese."

Playing with food
During the evening meal, musicians sometimes played to entertain. After the guests had eaten they began to dance.

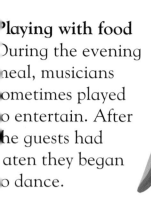

A hornpipe was a popular choice of instrument for a 15th-century musician.

Marriage
Noble women married young – some at the age of 14! Marriages were arranged to increase power and wealth.

people enjoyed live music, games, and dance.

A busy life
A lady of the castle was supposed to spin wool and sew, and run the kitchens and living quarters. She also had to receive and entertain guests, and take charge of running the castle if her husband was away.

The queen of the castle

Dining and hunting

A castle's kitchen was a busy place. The "stove" was a huge open fireplace where meat was roasted and bread was baked in special ovens. Then servants ferried the dishes to the Great Hall.

Feast your eyes
Banquets were grand affairs with elaborate platters of roast boar, baked fish, and spicy pastries.

Most fresh fruits and vegetables came from the castle gardens.

Flat pieces of stale bread were used as plates.

Flying for fun
Most nobles loved to go "hawking" – hunting with hawks or falcons. It took great skill to train a wild bird to kill and then return to its master.

Hood

Bird blinders
The only way to keep a falcon from attacking every time it saw other birds was to blindfold it with a tiny hood. Just before being let loose, the hood was slipped off.

Not a glove puppet
A hawk handler wore thick leather gloves to prevent a hawk's sharp talons from cutting his hand.

A trained killer

Essential clothing

Short leather thongs, called jesses, were fastened to the bird's legs to keep it perched on a fist.

Tough leather glove

13

The castle killers

There are three ways to capture a castle: Demanding its surrender without a fight is the fastest. Starving out the defenders is the slowest. Battering down the walls with special machines is the hardest.

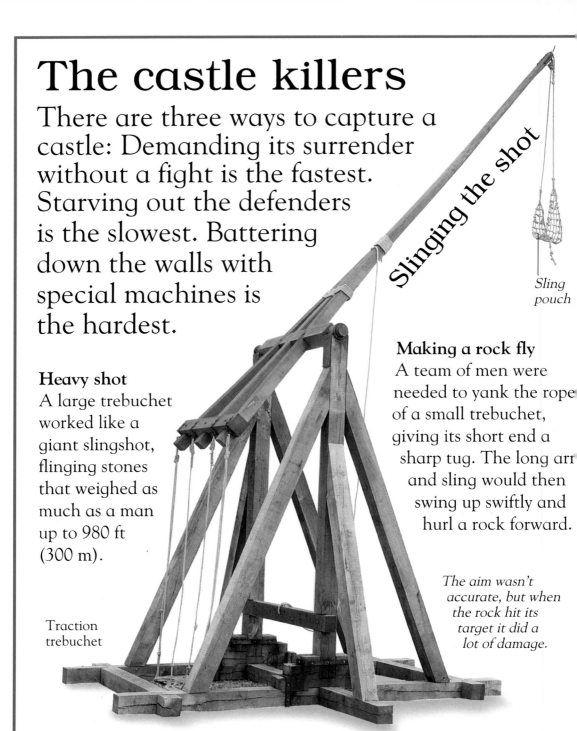

Slinging the shot

Sling pouch

Heavy shot
A large trebuchet worked like a giant slingshot, flinging stones that weighed as much as a man up to 980 ft (300 m).

Traction trebuchet

Making a rock fly
A team of men were needed to yank the rope of a small trebuchet, giving its short end a sharp tug. The long arm and sling would then swing up swiftly and hurl a rock forward.

The aim wasn't accurate, but when the rock hit its target it did a lot of damage.

Catapult

Twaaang!

The catapult had a short wooden arm with a cup at one end that could fling rocks, dead animals, flaming rags, and any other missiles that might make life miserable for the defenders.

Tunneling in

If a castle had no moat, attackers sometimes dug their way in under the walls – or they dug deep enough to make the walls collapse.

Ladders and movable seige towers could scale the castle walls.

Defenders had a good view of the enemy's movements from the turrets.

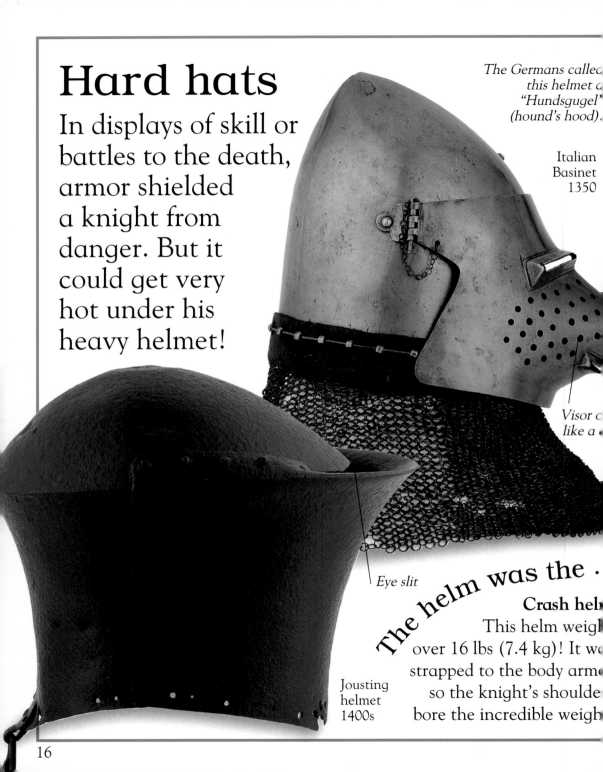

Hard hats

In displays of skill or battles to the death, armor shielded a knight from danger. But it could get very hot under his heavy helmet!

The Germans called
this helmet a
"Hundsgugel"
(hound's hood).

Italian
Basinet
1350

Visor c
like a

Eye slit

Jousting
helmet
1400s

The helm was the ·

Crash hel
This helm weigh
over 16 lbs (7.4 kg)! It w
strapped to the body arm
so the knight's shoulde
bore the incredible weigh

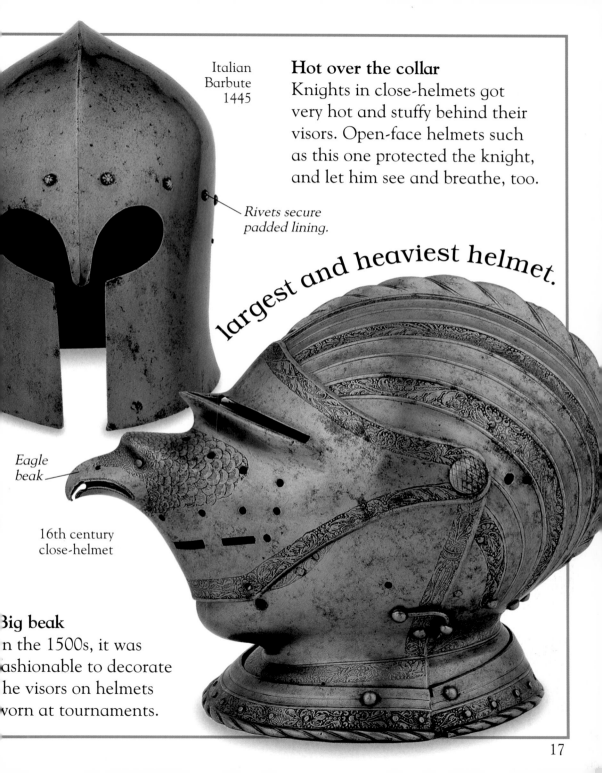

Italian
Barbute
1445

Hot over the collar
Knights in close-helmets got
very hot and stuffy behind their
visors. Open-face helmets such
as this one protected the knight,
and let him see and breathe, too.

*Rivets secure
padded lining.*

largest and heaviest helmet.

*Eagle
beak*

16th century
close-helmet

Big beak
In the 1500s, it was
fashionable to decorate
the visors on helmets
worn at tournaments.

Flashing blades

Knights used swords. A big two-edged cutting
sword was wielded by slashing it from side to
side. Pointed swords could
be stabbed into the joints
in an opponent's armor.

The sword ...

Ceremonial
sword

Scottish claymore

Highlander two-hander!
This two-handed Scottish claymore
was made around 1620, and
used in the Scottish highlands.
"Claymore" means "great sword."

sword could cut

Two-handed sword

*Lugs prevented
enemy weapons
from sliding down
the blade.*

The two-handed

Holy stab wounds

Indian holy men were not supposed to carry traditional weapons, so instead this dagger blade was hidden inside a walking stick.

Indian steel dagger

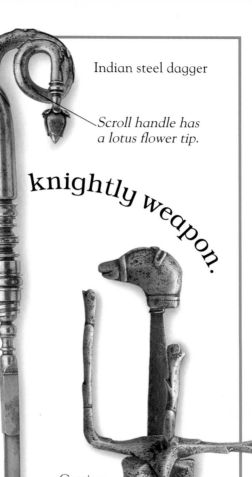

Scroll handle has a lotus flower tip.

was the most important **knightly weapon.**

This two-handed sword was probably used in ceremonies.

Strong arm methods

Soldiers had to be strong to swing two-handed swords. They were the biggest swords used and packed a terrific punch.

Cutting sword

rough **mail and bone!**

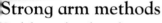

The pike slicer

This sword was made with a wavy edge to lop off the heads of long pikes carried by foot soldiers.

Single-edged sword

Bows and arrows

Mounted soldiers feared attack from foot soldiers armed with longbows and crossbows. Swift arrows could bring down horses and pierce the thickest armor.

Guns were not as powerful as crossbows until the 1800s.

Power of the bow

A 14th-century crossbow was so powerful it could kill a man at 650 ft (200 m).

Crossbows were slow to load

but easy to shoot

This bow was so strong, it had to be loaded with a crank.

A steel tipped bolt for war

A wide-headed bolt for hunting

The arrow (called a bolt) fitted in this groove.

Bolt from the blue

When a steel-tipped bolt from a crossbow hit iron armor straight on and at close range, it could punch a hole right through it.

Lots of practice

It took years of practice to fire a longbow well. Great strength was needed to manage a pull of at least 80 lbs (36 kg).

A longbow was as tall as an archer.

Arrow shafts were made from birch or ash wood. The flights were goose feathers.

Longbows were carved from a single piece of wood.

Rain of death

Good longbowmen could fire 12 arrows a minute, sending a storm of arrows through the air. Their biggest problem was running out of arrows during a battle.

Riding to war

A knight needed a horse to ride into battle, as well as for hunting, jousting, and carting all of his possessions. Most knights had several horses.

Most knights could only afford head armor ...

Proud steed
This 16th-century horse armor was made to protect a horse's head and neck. The metal has been decorated with etchings of birds and animals.

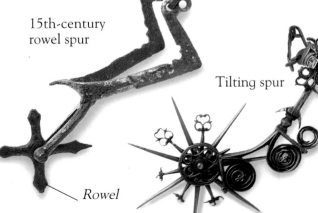

15th-century rowel spur

Tilting spur

Spurred on
Jousting knights had spurs with a rotating spiked wheel or rowel to urge their horses to charge each other.

Rowel

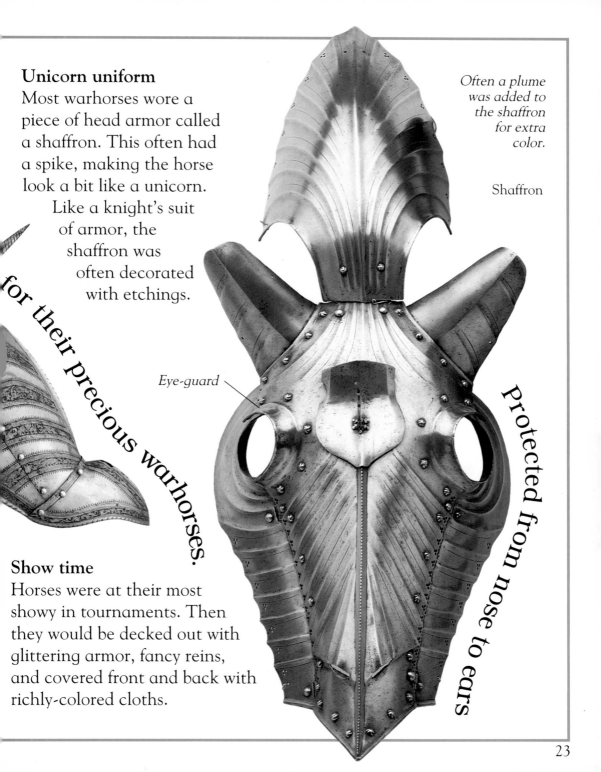

Unicorn uniform

Most warhorses wore a piece of head armor called a shaffron. This often had a spike, making the horse look a bit like a unicorn. Like a knight's suit of armor, the shaffron was often decorated with etchings.

Often a plume was added to the shaffron for extra color.

Shaffron

Eye-guard

for their precious warhorses.

Protected from nose to ears

Show time

Horses were at their most showy in tournaments. Then they would be decked out with glittering armor, fancy reins, and covered front and back with richly-colored cloths.

Lance a lot

In the 1200s, mock battles, or tourneys, were fought between teams on horseback. The highlight was a joust – a battle between two mounted knights.

a blunted lance

A knight used

Clash of stee
The knight
clashed s
heavily tha
sometime
the horses wer
knocked over

Full tilt
In the 1400s, barriers called tilts were set up to stop the charging horses from colliding. Special tilting armor protected the knights.

Family colors
Each knight had his own family crest marked on his shield, his tunic, and even on the cloth covering his horse. This was known as a coat of arms.

to try to push his opponent to the ground.

Wooden lances splintered easily on impact.

Tilting at a tournament

In some jousts the knights would dismount and continue the battle with swords.

25

Staying alive

A suit of armor protected a knight from head to toe.

Heavy head

A helmet usually weighed between 3 to 7 lbs (1½ to 3 kg). It was lined for comfort and had a chin strap to keep it from flying off in battle.

Movable visor

A shell fit to take serious punishment.

Collar plate to protect the neck.

Plated armor around waist allowed easy movement.

Elbow guard

Shoulder armor fitted over the breast and back plates.

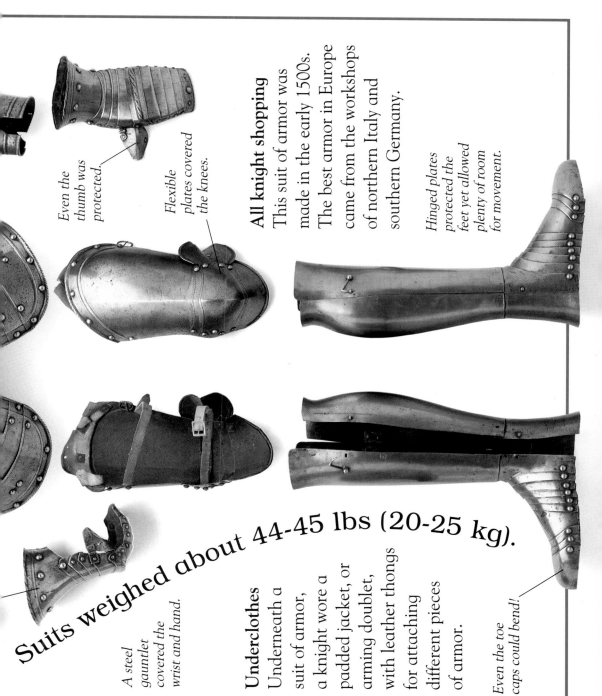

Even the thumb was protected.

Flexible plates covered the knees.

All knight shopping
This suit of armor was made in the early 1500s. The best armor in Europe came from the workshops of northern Italy and southern Germany.

Hinged plates protected the feet yet allowed plenty of room for movement.

Suits weighed about 44-45 lbs (20-25 kg).

A steel gauntlet covered the wrist and hand.

Underclothes
Underneath a suit of armor, a knight wore a padded jacket, or arming doublet, with leather thongs for attaching different pieces of armor.

Even the toe caps could bend!

World at war

Many ingenious weapons have appeared around the world. These deadly axes and vicious blades prove that there was no lack of imagination when it came to inventing weird weapons of war.

Tiger claw

Not even safe to shake hands
Tigers in India gave local people a gruesome idea for this hand weapon called a tiger claw.

Not one to throw away
This African throwing knife from Zaire spun as it flew. No matter which side hit, it was bound to do a lot of damage.

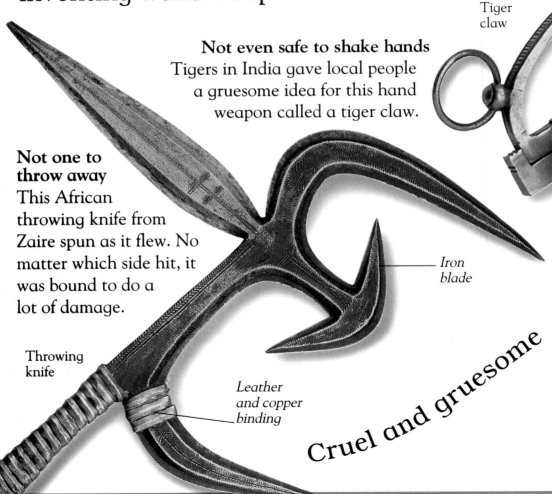

Iron blade

Throwing knife

Leather and copper binding

Cruel and gruesome

Chop, hack, slash

Wrist knife

Covered cutting edge

Armed arms
This circular wrist knife was worn in
Kenya. The razor-sharp edge is covered
to make it safer to handle.

weapons from around the world.

*One spike
always points
upward.*

Caltrop

Don't drop that caltrop
Caltrops, or crow's feet, were
four-pointed spikes that were
thrown on the ground to
cripple charging horses.

*Three spikes rest
on the ground.*

Index

Five chivalrous questions

1) On what level was the door to a keep

2) What kind of skirts did knights wear?

3) Who was in charge of a castle if a knight was away?

4) What was a knight doing if he was "hawking?"

5) What kind of slingshot could knock down castle walls?

  (a) a rockenroll
  (b) a catapult
  (c) a gondola
  (d) a trebuchet
  (e) a flingula

Answers on page 32

Who would have lived in a place like this?

Answers

From page 30:

1. The door was on the second floor
2. Mail armor skirts around the middle
3. The lady of the castle
4. Hunting with a hawk or falcon
5. A trebuchet

From page 31: A German lord lived in this castle along the Rhine River during the Middle Ages. From here he commanded a great stretch of river.